Also available in the series:

Eve Names the Animals by Susan Donnelly
Rain by William Carpenter
This Body of Silk by Sue Ellen Thompson
Valentino's Hair by Yvonne Sapia
The Holyoke by Frank Gaspar
Dangerous Life by Lucia Maria Perillo

The Morse Poetry Prize
Edited by Guy Rotella

J. ALLYN ROSSER

Bright
Moves

THE 1990 MORSE
POETRY PRIZE
🖋 SELECTED AND
INTRODUCED BY
CHARLES SIMIC

Northeastern University Press
BOSTON

Northeastern University Press

Library of Congress Cataloging-in-Publication Data

Rosser, J. Allyn, (Jill Allyn), 1957–
    Bright moves : the 1990 Morse Poetry Prize / J. Allyn Rosser ;
Selected and Introduced by Charles Simic.
    p.   cm.
    ISBN 1-55553-083-4 (acid-free)
    I. Simic, Charles, 1938–   II. Title.
PS3568.O8466B7   1990
811'.54—dc20   90-41407

Designed by Ann Twombly

Composed in Weiss by Eastern Typesetting Company, South Windsor, Connecticut. Printed and bound by McNaughton & Gunn, Saline, Michigan. The paper is Glatfelter Offset, an acid-free sheet.

MANUFACTURED IN THE UNITED STATES OF AMERICA
95 94 93   5 4 3 2

For my mother and father,
and for Shellie

On est quelquefois aussi différent de soi-même que des autres.

—La Rochefoucauld

ACKNOWLEDGMENTS

Grateful acknowledgment is made to the editors of the following publications, in which these poems first appeared, some in slightly different form: *Crazyhorse*: "The Quickness of Things." *The Georgia Review*: "Goose's Jack: Over the Hill?" "Last I Remember: 1973," "Letter to the Cracker Company," "Manichean Middle Game," "Ode on the Unsung." *The Gettysburg Review*: "Love Lessons." *The Hudson Review*: "Getting Wise," "An Open Fire," "What Was Clear." *Negative Capability*: "Equitable Distribution," "Premeditation." *New England Review*: "A Dream of Ezra Pound." *Paris Review*: "The City Underneath," "A sense of connection, as in." *Poetry*: "Advice to the Unadvisable," "Clippings," "The Dropping of a Name," "In the (Subjunctive) Mood," "My Father's Palette," "Remains," "Soundtrack of a Desert Documentary," "Timeline." *Poetry Northwest*: "Message: Bottle #32."

"Advice to the Unadvisable," "Clippings," "Remains," and "Timeline" won the Frederick Bock Prize from *Poetry*.

The passage by Alain Robbe-Grillet on page 43 is quoted from an interview in *Paris Review* 99 (Spring 1986).

The author would also like to thank the Corporation of Yaddo and the New Jersey State Council on the Arts for their generous support during the writing of this book.

Special thanks to Daniel Hoffman, teacher and friend.

Contents

Introduction

We don't know who was the first, Sappho, or some long forgotten contemporary of hers, but in the seventh century B.C. we hear something completely new in poetry, a voice and a manner which is still with us. All of a sudden, as it were, instead of the stories of gods and heroes, we have the life of the poet. No longer what Zeus and Achilles did, but what some woman on an island off Asia Minor felt on a particular night when she couldn't sleep and the sky was full of stars. Her loves, her losses, her own unique moment of existence are now the subject of poetry.

This is the beginning of lyric poetry as it is still practiced today. Its appearance represents a great change in the history of literature as well as the history of consciousness. It marks the shift from a mythologized to a realistic view of the world. It is in such poems that the literary universe is inhabited for the first time by individuals. Of course, there was lyric poetry before that, folk songs sung by men and women, but their speakers and their stories were anonymous. Sappho inserts the first person pronoun. The story of her solitude becomes the story of all our solitudes.

I was reminded of this long tradition reading J. Allyn Rosser's poems. She, too, is a part of that tradition. She writes of her experience, or rather she tells stories, stories about men and women, fathers and daughters, and she tells them well. Perhaps I should say she hears them well? For how can one tell a story in a poem if one doesn't hear what the language does on the page? And she does! Her ear in these poems is as fine as a musician's.

Reading her I was also reminded that in poetry the narrative proceeds by daring leaps. One cannot put everything in a poem, so the poet is forced to make choices. Such choices—the parts that one decides will stand for the missing whole—are the soul of the poetry. In such choices we recognize the poet's distinctness, the poet's "vision," as in these concluding lines to Rosser's poem "Last I Remember: 1973."

> It was that night, I'm sure—
> at least it was for me—
> but when did we first
> stand apart? The crowd
> began to yield distinct
> faces of solitary men we saw
> separately. Last I remember,
> the barker had tipped his hat
> and come away; he wanted
> to open the tent of your dress,
> or mine,
> and was willing to pay.

Another reason for telling stories is to make sense of one's experience. Narrative demands coherence. It is a challenge to our experience. (This is true of love poems, too.) In order to find order we have to look at life from a distance—as if it were a painting, a painting with figures in it.

Interestingly, in a poem called "My Father's Palette," the poet asks her father why there aren't any people in his landscapes. His reply is that "you don't have to see people to know they've been there."

Rosser has painterly instincts. She takes experiences one at a time, frames them. Her predilection is toward a kind of impressionism; not so much what is there, but what it feels like. The mouth tells stories, the eye only wants to see. The poems are full of finely observed and composed scenes.

The result of all this is a first book of uncommon excellence and promise. There's a love of clarity in these poems, a precision, the need to put each word in its proper place. There's also wit and humor and imagination. The poems are entertaining, and that's how it ought to be. It's not only the truth of experience that poets wish to convey with their stories. They also want to give pleasure. *Bright Moves* is a book of many pleasures.

CHARLES SIMIC

I

◈ The City Underneath

—for T.Š.

I.

There is a woman living inside
that man, deep in his chest, almost
in spite of his life. She is beautiful
and sleeps all day, barely stirring or breathing,
though you'd never know it to look at him. Go on. Closer.
Note the jawline. He has developed a thicker, roughened skin
that keeps her in.

II.

You'd never guessed? There is another
underneath—nothing like this one, with these
flattened beer cans studding the gutters. They have
none of our poorly painted women, wan men, fearful odors.
They walk on lawn, among lilacs. Fountains. They smile to see
one another, and can be heard singing softly in the street beneath
the one we're on.

III.

Stand very still some coolish evening.
See if you can't grasp the extra galaxy past
the last one visible on clearest nights—don't look
for anything. Let your eyes go completely out of your head.
Just make sure it's dark, cool. Stand very still. Look at me,
my eyes, if that will help. The words I really want to say to you
are under these.

✺ My Father's Palette

I thought I understood what it was for,
like an unopened box of crayons.
It was always in the window room
with the splattered linoleum floor,
even when he wasn't. It was exciting,
like Felix the Cat's bag of tricks,
the primary splotches blending
one day in swirls of autumn russet—
the next in summer camembert
or winter's whited blues.
Or smeared, first muddy, then clear
with the molted rags of my youth
he soaked in that Lethean turpentine,
a stench that washed all colors
back to scratch: to the brown wood,
the kidney-shaped monument
to every vista he'd sold, or given,
or wordlessly stacked in the attic.
I liked to put my thumb in its thumb-hole,
or to see it humped with rigid blobs
left over from the day before,
when calmly as a surgeon in Emergency
he'd slit the skins—cerulean
or sepia—apply freshly oozing hues
to the erection of skewed fenceposts
enclosing his fields of revision:
all those long-abandoned barns,
complicated trees,
desolate plainscapes . . .

But no people. Growing up
I couldn't fathom why he left them out,
always straining to glimpse

the profile of a human head
through the glare of his blank windows,
trying to see
what he saw
in uninhabitably old farmhouses,
fallow fields. When I asked, once,
he nodded and said something
I can't exactly remember:
how you didn't have to see people
to know they'd been there,
or could have been, and when I still
didn't get it, he fell silent,
vaguely disappointed.
I never asked again.

He probably thinks I still don't
understand. But I remember
that time in Bermuda when, drowsy,
pretending to be asleep on the ugly
plaid couch of my parents' hotel room,
I watched my father quietly take in
all that was missing
in the mass-produced hotel painting.
I remember the boring waves
spraying over the boring rocks
on the wall, and with what restraint
he selected the skinniest brushes
and the tubes for fleshtone
and for swimsuit crimson, stirring
on a tinfoil takeout plate.
And the placing of the lamp.
And how the smoke from his pipe
my mother didn't mind that night
drifted across and above
his intent frame as he bent

away from us in silhouette
to add, with minute strokes,
two faroff figures—maybe lovers—
to the utterly featureless water.
How he added always the human
when we couldn't find it in everything.

✺ *Last I Remember:* 1973

It was back before consequence
was a word, back
in that sticky dark town
that July when we snuck
without tickets or shame
over fences and wet fields
that sopped us all the way
up to our womaning thighs:
giggling, giddy and slipping
where earlier elephants
had walked off their fodder—
   Stinking then!
like a circus ourselves
we weaseled through the flap
and into the gawking crowds,
the tawdry light—oh, stinking
with this royal adolescence
smeared on our lips,
and swinging our hips
the way we dared to then,
not touching but joined
somehow, side by side,
sharing the hilt of that
jaunty cutlass wit
we'd sharpened on silly boys
who didn't need their razors yet;
sharing too the lifted chin,
the jungle tan, we circled
the cages of tigers
who circled after us,
unhinged at our heckling,
who spat and rolled their r's
and untamed eyes

(what in us did they recognize?)
while the whole hometown
whispered and hissed:
attention we sought and got
and craved and sought again,
suspended in the grace
of unconcern, that summertime
of repercussionless éclat,
all impulse and act,
prancing on the fat zero
of our timeline,
the force of innocence
holding us back like the rope
for the horses' redoppe,
allowing only that ten-foot radius,
cantering circles that never
broke stride or broke
from that fantastic
ring of light . . .

It was that night, I'm sure—
at least it was for me—
but when did we first
stand apart? The crowd
began to yield distinct
faces of solitary men we saw
separately. Last I remember,
the barker had tipped his hat
and come away; he wanted
to open the tent of your dress,
or mine,
and was willing to pay.

◝ Getting Wise

In the same extreme summer, after walking
smartly away from college
only to learn I was incapable of lying
believably about having waitressed
plenty of times before
in lots of different places,
I took a job at the plastics factory
and had all four wisdom teeth
pulled at once.

Even then I think I knew it for cliché,
the implausible dream of the privileged—
but I had a real desire to feel my own salt
soak into the back of my shirt
all day alongside nonunionized
Puerto Ricans and Vietnamese; like them
to hold my tongue and bow down
to machinery that wouldn't stop;
to refuse the earplugs that didn't help;
to feel and share their powerlessness.
And I felt I *did* feel it, with all
the fierce authority of uttering
one's first profoundly earned "Goddammit!"
slamming those sharp-edged meat trays
into accordions taut enough for boxes.
The heat in there was unholy.
My inner forearms ripped to bleeding.
Of course it didn't matter
how hard I tried, the others always knew
I could walk out when I pleased—
and all their broken speeches mended
just enough to say so. For fun,
the foreman cranked the rollers

into double-time at my station.
I nearly bit my lip right through
to keep up. It seemed important
to eat those cardboard sandwiches
from the vending machine,
and to keep from coughing
when the plastic fumes were all
we had to breathe.

The joke wore off, my trays slowed down,
and a few of the women began vaguely
to include me in breakroom conversation.
The men lent me change, and displayed
photos of children in glass-beaded braids
and ill-fitting Sunday clothes.
Still they wouldn't smile all the way
or look me right in the eye.
Not until I showed up that Wednesday
after the extractions, grotesquely
swollen with blue-yellow bruises
along my jaw and under my eyes,
would Fatima acknowledge my presence:
"Your boyfriend—he do this?"
Everyone at the table was staring.
"Well," I said, half-whispering,
and then: "He has a terrible temper."
The women nodded. The men shook their heads.
I thought I could live with a lie so small.
But Thursday morning Jojo greeted me
with rice cakes, and Conchita
explained about her husband in California.
Cheng-Liu showed me how to stack boxes
so they'd never fall, and invited me
home to dinner some day soon. I said
I'd come, and really should have

come back for my check the next day.
I needed them to believe something of me,
at least that I needed the money.
Instead I sponged St. Tropez Bronze
over the bruises, coiled my hair
in a chignon, put on pearls
and long-sleeved silk, walked
into the best restaurant in town
and told the manager yes,
years and years in every kind of place,
you name it: Chinese cuisine, Italian, French.
I smiled right in his face.
I got the job. It was easy.

⚜ Clippings

As usual, the postman has crumpled
my bouquet of obligations.
I pluck out the one envelope
addressed in a long familiar hand:
another batch of clippings
from my mother. Not even a note
enclosed, as if she's embarrassed
to have me know she sent them:
smudgy news of people I used to know,
or things I really ought to know
by now: articles on lowered interest rates,
what to do with leftover egg whites,
the disastrous effects of caffeine
on nervous systems like mine.
Things I squint at briefly, or toss
aside for the books she claims—
"so thin!"—I seem to live on.
Like a wasp, I quip when I call
this afternoon, to be corrected:
"Wasps live *in* paper, not on it.
They eat the worms that eat
our cabbages back home."
Naturally. What do I know? "You?
You cut your teeth on cloth-bound books."
As if this too were news. I know,
I know, but really I want
not to be impatient, want badly

to be the once-blind beautiful girl
in the Chaplin film who sees
for the first time, through a shop window,
some flop-footed bum on the street
who has starved to pay for her operation.

She doesn't know. She mouths a word
or two, and gestures, points down,
he has dropped his beat-up flower,
and he looks down, and up again;
the two of them performing
the doubly silent feature of strangers
through windows. He is bashful,
dazzled by her newly sighted kindness:
a long slow smile. She motions him
to the door, meets him with a fresh flower,
and a coin she presses into his palm—
Buy yourself some coffee, we must lipread,
though the glass no longer separates them—
She knows the hand! She clutches it
in both of hers, tearfully. You? *You?*

I haven't been listening. She refrains
from saying there will be something
on wasps in the forthcoming nest
of newsprint. I won't be surprised.
But maybe next time, slowly tracing
the crowded words with my finger,
which looks so much like her finger,
I'll know which words are hers, and follow
closely, quietly along, mouthing back
that long slow smile I've grown up
mouthing off to. Right now, I tell her,
I have to go. I thank her for today's
week-old clippings which I surely
will get to sometime, maybe read them
later on, when it starts to get dark,
ruin my eyes.

⚜ The Making of a Scruple

And in all the land were no women found
so fair as the daughters of Job.
—Job 42:15

While aphids and toads were safe,
being good and ugly, ladybugs
not only groomed our garden
but looked stunning on my knee
or on my sister's wrist,
and so we had to have each one
we saw. First aligning one finger
with the grass blade or shingle it labored
to climb, we'd softly angle,
guide, nudge it to the landscape
of the other hand, so gently
it wouldn't even think to lift
its crimson, popcorn-skin-thin
wing sheaths for flight. Each move
was calculated not to feel
like more than normal danger.
With held breath and steady eyes,
we watched our creatures blunder
into subtly planned frustrations,
confusions, vague hells
of flesh desert and knuckle mountain;
a gentle torture, like loving
the stuffing out of teddy bears
by hugging them too hard.

The day comes when each of us
is overloved, whether by a god
or mortal father, or a man.
Now I shoo the sweet bright beetles

14

that land in their innocence
too temptingly near my hand
since the time I felt the whole
entrusted body of my life
lurch and pivot for footing
as if on an outstretched palm
suddenly turned vertical;
and since I've stopped at walls
made by the fascinated hands
of lovers whose whims became needs
that grew to block my own—
a trammeling so soft and sweet
it could not trip the soul's alarm—
as slowly I turned round
and round again beneath
the great cold slab of sky
lowered like a slate-colored eye
much too close to mine,
mocking my next bright move.

◢ A Dream of Ezra Pound

I'd eaten dark chocolate, reading late at night.
   They introduced me, and I still hadn't read
   All the *Cantos*. Somehow he knew this on sight.

Still, his large old hand shook mine; I stayed
   With him to kiss that wistful dented cheek;
   He was shyly pleased, beard glowing, and said:

(I couldn't hear. His voice was oddly weak,
   As if it came from behind him.) Police
   Were there. He'd come back down, or up, to speak

On God. So he was not completely at ease
   When my colleagues nattered on and on
   About their flatly mispronounced *bêtises;*

But he was polite—extremely—to everyone!
   Had he learned the hard way from his hard bed
   In Saint Elizabeths, lying endlessly alone,

To nod when it was necessary to nod? He did.
   It went over well with the academicians,
   Beamish boys. At last he shook his head—

His voice resumed the vibrant hallowing insistence
   I'd expected, though much softer, bereaved,
   In broken response to some jargonous nonsense:

"Yes yes, we think in order to know, or perceive—
   And in this we are sometimes, it seems, successful—
   But we *believe* in order to *believe.*"

He said this in worn sorrow, in sorrow distressful
   He said this, E.P., with no madness up his sleeve.
   "No god," he said. "Nothing but what we may leave."

⤜ Manichean Middle Game

I.

Say instead of there is
No god, instead of
Dozens of deities concocting
Ambrosial or splenetic schemes,
Or just One,
Or Three-in-One,
Or a universal godinus;

Say rather there are
Two, discrete and equal,
Luxuriously quarrelsome:
One robed in black, One white,
Who sit at their checkered
Tablecloth in the sky
On a cosmic plane
Too fast for us to board
Or see . . .

A Tweedle-Dum and -Dee,
A cannier Shem and Shaun
Who've never been known
To nod or yawn
Over celestial Old-fashioneds;
But who, mutually opposed,
Mootly enthused, conjure
Constantly these versions
Of you and me.
Say the White One nearly
Always wins in the end,
Surprising the hell
Out of the Black, who shiftily
Insists on keeping score.

A perpetual Katzenjammer
Twosome, then, making light
Of misery and joy
In forms of two,
Each rending the too-
Beautiful fabrics of the other,
Allotting intricate cruelties
And unjust rewards;
Sowing and reversing
Convictions
For the sheer delight
Of moving the pieces
Back and forth between them.

II.

Let me say here and now I love
You above all, knowing you
Know I've loved others
For much longer, when much
Younger; and grant that you
Believe me utterly,
Responding in kind,
Muffling your yesses
Against mine; and let us pray
There will not be any
Other one for you but me,
For me but you, and Hey!
Let's make exclusive,
Juicy love on white sheets
In a room of shifting
Square shadows, until
We're 89 or 93, imagining
Constantly that this is where
We both most want to be . . .

III.

Your move, Soot-face.

The skinny, whiskered One in black
Takes a queen with his pawn
   and leans back,
Laughing: *Bliss is for saps.*
The fat One scratches his horn
   and smiles: *Perhaps.*

II

〰 Love Lessons

It's the one thing
you have to learn
not to learn too well.

You don't have to dress up.
You can't bring
anyone else.

The rules are variable;
the winnings, subjective.
And it's never

over. Even if you cheat.
Even if you walk out, roll again,
leave the country.

The strategy is always the same:
give and let give.
It's simple. Everyone forgets.

One more thing.
If you worry about getting taken,
you will get taken.

If you give up worrying,
then
you have been taken.

✒ Goose's Jack: Over the Hill?

*No one in the folk-lore sense climbs to the top of a hill
for water unless that water has special significance.*
—Lewis Spence

Something, then—a stain on her dress,
a bee in her bonnet, the last stick
of gum unshared—something has been
left out. Perhaps he wasn't all he'd been
cracked up to be. On this point
the text is clearly ambiguous.
But you're not going to tell me
Jack simply "fell" down. Okay,
let's say she never actually pushed him.
The word *fell* is the ticket here.
Fell: fierce. *Fell,* closely echoing
fail. Jack *failed* to find water.
He failed *fiercely,* the way they do.
I'm not saying I don't sympathize.
But you can't overlook the fact
that *fell* slant-rhymes ever so wantonly
with *Jill,* suggesting that Jack has connected
        Jill and *fail*
inextricably in his man-mind,
that feckless projector of choppy
home movies where the heads
of the beloved are cut off,
their least fetching sides exposed.
So if Jack is the determinist hero
of Jill's self-actualized world-view,
it follows that Jack was not totally
at fault in his wish-fulfilling
falling. It is readily inferable
that what really went down

was Jack's confidence in his
water-finding abilities:
a slip of the old divining rod,
a "tumble" curtailed. Of course
we can only speculate.

✒ Post-thalamion

I. An Open Fire

I would not trace your steps
from here to all the world
and back—but there are dusks
that fall without you
when the gaslight will not catch
and I can sense your eyes on others,
pick up the scent of smiles
they cast on you. I concentrate
on flame, make dinner glow.

Later, you tend the blue light
of the evening news
strobing our overheated den
and lean closer
as if quickened by disaster,
rapt in a fabulous safety:
leaking toxins, gagging streams
and all the unsafe elsewhere
you, by watching, make stay there—

like the first man on earth
watching darkness through an open fire
at the mouth of his cave.
What he cannot quite make out
won't hurt *us*,
though it pass near enough
to fling fantastic shadow,
ripple through alerted blood
and lick the thinning, blackened air,
this flimsy air before us.

II. *Kiss Me You Fool*

Down on all fours, the morning after
your demon has scratched
the eyes out of mine,

I grope on the rug
for lost pieces of things,
some of them yours.

Your roses on the coffee table
level with me, sick
of craning their necks

over baby's breath
and bad language. They stick
all their tongues out at once.

Clearly they can't keep
putting up with this,
having gone to such crooked

lengths to be only beautiful, only
to die with flying colors.
You walk in, unshaven, just

as I find two petals, still
red, shaped like hearts.
Almost like hearts.

The height of passion's a cinch
to reach. Then what? A breeze
too strong for ripened parts?

III. *What Was Clear*

After the old friends and the new friends
and all the other guests were gone,
we sat at the table for hours
pondering contour and color,
forcing parts to interlock
and then thinking
better of it, thinking
maybe the puzzle was not
one, but two in one box.

No picture there to clue us in.
Still, edges were quickly complete
with corners and the usual sky.
On one side, the red of a barn
you called schoolhouse;
on the other, my cypress—
your oak. We squinted
and pressed, irritable
and hopeless by turns.

There was a lagoon at last,
with something there floating,
surely swans. But you laughed:
ducks. A white rowboat
after all, with a gap inside,
and something gray and something red
(two pieces we would never find).
A rag and a bucket, you said.
But it was a child with a pail.

IV. *Separation: Summer Night*

So I unto my selfe alone shall sing,
The woods shall to me answere and my Eccho ring.
            —Spenser, *Epithalamion*

Tonight the lamplight holds me derelict
at my desk, mocks me in yellow colors,
and sends a wire to every errant insect
within acres. I will screen such callers,
dismiss the Muses, brace each door that hinges
inward. There, love. I'll visit upon our honor
no reflection, but commune with what cringes
and crawls: all the clambering damned with torn or
hardened antennae, who've come so far to press
their tiny souls against the screen, grasping
at my little light, poor mecca of redress
for poorest mortals. Look: flattened, gasping,
they bear their flagging wings intact, and fight
to keep that tiny sense of self upright.

🖎 Equitable Distribution

In the mall of ever after and true love
We separate and shop around, aghast,
For things we never thought of getting two of.

Dodging jewelers we'd once played the fool of,
Prowling racks past season, thinking fast
In the mall of ever after and true love,

We browse through needs the other never knew of,
Inspect, and drastically discount, the past
We never once thought we'd make two of.

Let's each trade rings for one more turtle dove
And break whatever bonds cannot be cashed
In the mall of ever after and true love.

I'll keep the house and child in lieu of you, love.
You keep the car and all the photographs
We never did think to take two of.

Before our overheated hearts cool off,
We'll beat them back in shape to be recast
In the mall of ever after for more true love,
One thing we never thought we would need two of.

🍃 Premeditation

The TV is on, going on
about something: a man leaving
a woman, a woman a man.
A storm lashes at the window
I watch them watching.
Their lively voices rise, clashing
in expert rage and desperation,
all the shrillness rehearsed
out of them; the scene headlong,
spliced clean of dead air.

When the phone rings, it will be
your voice going on about me,
mine about you. On either end
we'll twine the cord around
our fingers and speak in turn,
in even tones, addressing our
difficult question. Silence
will intervene where it can,
raising its hand with the answer.
We'll hang up just in time

to pick up where the woman
and man will give in and sink
back together, the problem unresolved.
They'll make love right on top of it!
So when they get up it won't look
like the same problem at all.
Something to be said for this,
making hard questions easy
not to answer, like equations
in a Teacher's Edition, the pink pages
eager as tongues to explain.

༄ The Quickness of Things

How suddenly the heart recoils
from what it's fed on for fourteen years:
embraces stiffen, heads avert,
and for what? One day the taste of something
just sickens—the scrambled eggs will not stay
down, and the rest of your life you avoid
anything to do with chickens. Or say
the spacious ash-blue boring sky
of August turns black! blotted out
by endless avenues of geese that lengthen
out of nowhere, where the geese
have been slowly gathering.
And even in a particularly sticky
season of heat, it can take less
than a second for air to come clean,
sweet among smatters of rain.
Of course it's been coming all along,
that's what gets you, and this time
you're standing in an overly familiar
crowded room when this distinctly new face
appears, Cheshire-style; no warning
this will be the core of your known
universe from now on, on into marriage
and so on until you one day discover
how few seconds it takes your now
husband, who knows you didn't really mean
what you just said, to say what
makes you wince or sob for years
until you leave him abruptly for no one
after washing the dishes, even then
wondering whether he meant it, whether
maybe you *should* have meant
what provoked it. There's no telling

how proudly you can carry sorrow
for months, months, not stooping
to spill a drop,
and one night it's too late
for the news, a movie comes on—
maudlin beyond belief, with formulaic
mournful speeches, rueful gazes,
boats that are missed or, worse,
taken, handkerchiefs waving
too late to be seen—and
there, now you're crying.
How quickly then your heart recalls
what it forgot.
                    How soon after
someone is shaking you by the shoulder:
Wake up, wake up, you're in love with me!
And sure enough it's true;
for a year or two This is it,
coffee and smiles all day Sunday,
this is the life; this is
the morning you're calmly getting out
of your paid-for Pontiac and there's
the corner of a note wedged in the crease
of the seat, the anonymous note
you've been sitting on blithely
for who knows how long. You reach down
and hope it's not for you.
(It's for you.)
                    So here come
the bad dreams, though you know
from experience that surely,
one day soon, the bad dreams, too,
will go. They go. For years
they're gone. How quickly then the gods
are heard to laugh, somewhere

very close to your face,
as they plant the impossible obstacle,
poise the last straw, fling
only the richest kind of mud—
like the peeled-off red sweatshirt
tossed wildly into your arms
by a child going by on his bike
for one more race downhill,
which becomes the last
warm thing of his you'll touch.

III

⫷ There Will Be Winters

when the dog sleeps in his clothes
   and all the world outside in tight
white scrolls of branch and log;

so cold your lips can't crack a smile
   without bleeding a little.
Dusk will sink into walls like a stain.

Even the footsteps in your pillow
   may cease. Outside the trees
will have drifted again, swooning

for the queenly moving snowfall
   that whispered nothings all night,
effacing self with more self.

You will dress silently, in layers,
   and dread the first green notion
that threatens to unfist your heart.

ᔥ *Solitary Figure, Adirondack Chair*

No one could sit that still for this long
without some utter saturation of peace
or nursed grief. From here, it's all one.
From here, it might be a woman or man or
tall child: just visible on the right is a corner
of elbow, unmoving, inscrutable, and between
five rough blue slats four tiny billowings
of white cotton—a round darkness just above;
above that the chair's scalloped top
and the flashing belt of lakewater, which might
be what she's staring at, if she's not reading,
and beyond it the arrangement of beaches and docks
and blueing browns of land on the opposite shore
where I live. And up an inch or so higher,
the fidgety green leaves of the maple rubbing
soundlessly against the curved inside
of the white porch roof, just starting to show
where the cracks will appear—fine smudgy veins
like those on a knocked-about hardboiled egg—
and the light fixture with its several dead moths.
Or she's tired. But the easy assumption being
that she's either deeply in love, or recently thrown
from it. A jilt would be the favored explanation,
since we'd expect some sign, jiggling knees,
tapping nails, bustling anxious gestures and tics,
if this were love's first flush—and it's no fun
to imagine the other kind, the mild neat composure
of insured affections older couples know. . . .
She's too young. And note the unsipped
condition of her tall drink, the melted cubes,
the slice of lemon undisturbed on the lip
of her glass. I'd say she's through with something
or someone. She's probably holding out, holding

her breath for some unplanned-for event, some
unexpected rescue from whatever this limbo is.
Or she's just looking at the water. From here,
I don't know what I am, can't remember
what I'm doing at the corner of her back lot
staring at her back porch and angled chair
overlooking her side of the lake, waiting
for the first move she'll make, the eventual
sigh sounding the depth from which she'll heave it.
What *is* she thinking, and of whom? What if I
approached her, loudly cracking twigs to prepare
for my intrusion—no, too softly for intrusion—
and demanded, in some as yet undiscovered
unthreatening charming manner she couldn't resist,
to *know*. I could tell you how I made her
turn, and how the gentle expression that fell
across her features made me feel, how she spoke
and what she said—her confidential tone—
but even then I would not know, and you
would never trust me there with her alone.

✐ In the (Subjunctive) Mood

Dear noun I'd never know, O man
of my dreams—I should really
like to keep you there,
honest, as far from my arms
as the one in the moon: round
white lie we love looking up to
without once stretching out a hand.

Even the moon must know better
than to touch down here,
where the wind at any moment
can slap a fond reflection
right out of the pond.
Lie easy where you are, obliquely
mine; off-center, but not wrong.

I'd wrap you in abstraction,
embed you in subplot, make you
the object of my wholly vocative O.
One quick call in the dead of night
had made a redoubtable prize,
a perfect present, of yourself:
voilà, the whites of your eyes; lo,

sighs drawn against my cheek.
If only these sheets were slips
of cloud, this telling breath a mist.
I think this time you'd best
put on your dream outfit for keeps—
it hides the better part of what
were better hid. Go back to sleep.

A flame lives longer in thin air,
these thousand miles between us.
Forget what you don't know. Stay there.

We'd want candles, wine and alibis
were this love merely in the making.
Let's keep this light, that might
go out with whispering, or waking.

◢ℯ Ode on the Unsung

Poor tongue, restless old clapper
tied to a watery bell,
forever doomed to depend
on the heart's impulse,
to founder on the unsound
advice of the head, and always
flubbing the signals,
getting in the way.

What tough luck
to be swollen with *mots justes*
it can almost taste
while the heart clangs one thing
and the head hammers another;
to be one caught between two
rows of teeth that never
meet in peace . . .

Poor solitary tongue, censored
and bound to seek solace
only in some other tongue:
absurd liaison that can only go
so far. They can never elope.
Still they wrestle and caress,
thinking *never, never,*
nevertheless.

✒ Advice for the Unadvisable

> It is not because a scene is important that it is
> repeated, but by being repeated it becomes
> important. In general, nothing really important
> happens in my films—it is the way certain scenes
> recur. As I said, there is no "significance."
> —Alain Robbe-Grillet

Recurrence often gives a heightened sense
Of life's mysteries. *Déjà vu* is news.
But you need not demand significance

Of insidiously similar events
Returning like a burden of the blues
Recurrence often gives. A heightened sense

Of what's beyond—to which the evidence
You're given offers few recurring clues—
That you need not demand. Significance

Is one myth every parent re-invents:
That old line, "Once upon a time," is a ruse
Whose very recurrence gives a heightened sense

Of each prince's uniqueness. Precedents,
However, are what real law-courts use . . .
But you need not. Demand significance

And ask for trouble. If everyone you love tends
To leave for the same reason, shrug. Learn to lose.
Such recurrence leaves us with a vague sense
That one need not demand significance.

🖋 Soundtrack of a Desert Documentary

The tumbleweed looks blue. It blows,
we know, by virtue of wind
   deaf to the skills
of Sibelius syncing along,
taking what's moving for dead,
   serial stills.

Without this music superadded
to our viewing screen
   of skidding weed,
would any of us gather here
that something passing lovely
   should be seen?

Surely wind and weed alone
make sound and sense enough
   for what they do.
We want to hear the tracks they make:
the rustle-hush, the mournful
   rising whoo,

drowned out by these subtitular whines,
this static intended to move us.
   We would like time
to hear ourselves think: *Wind. Weed.*
Your hand moving slowly
   over mine.

ᘯ Timeline

The first June I thought I would die of heartbreak
for a boy who didn't sufficiently appreciate a girl
who spent spare hours studying the section titled
"Stranger in Town" in *Spanish in a Nutshell* (¡Socorro!
¡Me han robado!) and *Practical Chinese Conversation*
(*Hsia-yu pu ch'ing-t'ien*, "It's not a fine day
when it rains"), you nearly died of spinal meningitis
in Paris. And when my car spun out of control
on the way back to college after seven months in Boston
as a dropout manqué, you were packing to move to Boston
where your life would become so rich with friends
and compatible intellects that you suspected marriage
was the logical next step on this ladder of happiness.
At the moment I decided to teach myself shorthand,
having dropped out for good for the second time,
you were working in the back of a bookstore
dreaming up a woman who could understand Nietzsche
in German, not once forgetting the z in his name,
and who could write you celebratory poems
that wouldn't sound tinny. And when I threw
my spiral dictation notebook at the fast-talking
TV anchorman, you were forgetting to remove
your red spiral notebook from a phone booth—
a loss you would mourn all your life. And it's true
that the week I entered law school you'd begun to look
at your wife's male friend with slightly altered eyes.
But is it possible that the frantic afternoon I decided
to quit law school for romantic reasons was the same day
you discovered you were drinking a beer you didn't want,
and feeling bored with marriage, or merely numb?
While I helped, more or less, to push my sister's car
up the blizzarded mountain in my wedding dress
you were upstairs in your father's house in Vermont

45

reading Kafka while everyone else was out skiing
in perfect conditions.

Wen shih ch'u tsai na-erh? Where is the information desk?
Chiu tsai ch'ien mien. It's right in front of us.

Of course, when I moved out that first summer,
under a shower of words hissed sharply enough
to be heard over all the neighbors' sprinklers, you
were still either bored or merely numb. And later
that same summer when I moved back in, carrying
grounds for divorce in the deepest pocket of my heart—
that's right, *moved back in,* an emotional gesture I still
can't swallow in retrospect, but have proof of—
you were writing about a mistress you didn't have.
And wasn't it *ta-hou-nien,* or "year after year after
the next," that I picked up the note left on my car seat
about the woman my husband had been lying about—
or so the note said—
just as you were thinking about not having children
for a while? Then the argument about his children
being his children, and the subsequent silent meal
I don't remember cooking or eating, at which moment
you were just carrying the window fan we still have
into your new apartment in the strange city
to which I would move the next time I left him.

ಜ್ Two Years Later

We meet in our respective best—
your tailored Italian suit, my dark blue dress
with raveling cuff—both of us a bit stiff
in gait and gesture, and kiss, still also
consciously dressed in the same flesh
we once mistook for ourselves. Our fingers
do not interlace. Preliminary words are exchanged,
throats cleared. You give me a look, and then
that look.
        I gaze firmly off at some indistinct point
in the restaurant—a button on a waiter's shirtfront—
groping for a lightly friendly neutral tone
that will not glaze over or freeze up
on the particulars you may dare to mention.
You do dare: a terrace in St. Croix,
a certain rooftop in October,
the last time we were "together"

and on that word you watch me slip into
my old rapid self-deprecating patter
which I now can see you helped me to perfect,
a habit I thought I'd overcome in my fine new life,
the one you haven't touched, and babble on
about my efforts to gain a "pathetic"
livelihood, and my (sunny, spacious) "low-rent"
apartment whose entryway I unnecessarily describe
as having a stained carpet the color of lima beans
or overcooked asparagus and an aroma I call
"essence of roach," but which is, despite
a slightly stale air of shabbiness, clean,
and on about what a jerk I am to have moved
into the very first place I'd seen (you nod),
and on with a list of successes I'm proud of

but which are minor enough to be rendered
convincingly in the light of failure.

The question remains, if our eyes moisten,
and will they, and whose, or whose first,—
what then? We pause for steaming plates,
you order more wine, and between cracks about
my culinary experiments and your eating habits,
we manage to get dinner down. Coffee.
Coffee. So. We square off at the table,
plates cleared, now I take a good look at your same
hair and eyes and mouth and all affection floods back
and patter ends. You are about to ask, now
you are asking the dreaded question, dreaded
because I've sensed in your steady serious interest
a greater sadness than mine, Am I, Can I say I am
happy? And I finger the possibility of saying,
for you, to give you something less bitter
to swallow, some form of *no;* I think of reservations
I might make up to mitigate my awful actual
yes that somehow I must now spit out,

and somehow do, looking at and even into your eyes,
I tell you I love my pathetic career, I do love it
and my low-rent slow-lane social life,
the subzero prestige in being literally lost to the world
in the stale air of pompous old books and though I hate
to hurt you I'm almost glad to be telling you this
because I can, through this forfeiture, this still
enormously painful failure to make you feel better,
better savor the fact that I *am* happy,
with my same lips I use this word in reference
to myself, I love the damn carpet and I love
all my appalling deprivations, not to mention
the equally hapless jerk I live with.

A sense of connection, as in

moments like this one, the green carpet
looking for once just the right green,
is it the lighting, or your shadow thrown
from the tan-and-rust couch where you sit lightly—
you seem in your reverie almost to hover—
clashing horridly in your incredible socks
with the magenta stripes above the sneakers
slashed by, even oozing with, crimson shoelaces;
and yes, to be completely honest, you're wearing
the T-shirt of yesterday. Orange stripes. But
I don't care, that is I love the angle
of your chin when you read and the color
of the shadow you throw without knowing it,
though even as I write, though I hate
to have to accept it just yet,
you've already begun to move, you've gone
into the kitchen, now calling softly to me
about a peach in the refrigerator, the mold
on the peach, asking me considerately do I want
to try to save it? and I'm touched,
a trifle puzzled but touched
and awed to the point of leaving my mouth open
to think that the color of it, the peach-mold,
probably exactly matches the precise hue
of the unshadowed carpet you've left me,
and I can safely say I'm delighted daily
with such unlooked-for symmetries as you
in your youness provide, all unwitting,
and I want to call softly back not just *No*,
let it go, but a harmonizing phrase, a signal
to bring you with a sudden smile in here
to evoke again that shadow on the carpet
that so often separates us, I'm actually craving

physically I think the even-toned, sturdy aquamarine
shadow that falls from the changeable zoo
of your otherness . . .
                              but you're very busy
washing, no rinsing something at the sink, no, now
chopping something harder than a peach,
I wonder if you'd even hear me, chopping in there,
chopping and chopping with disarming diligence
at the makings of a green salad.

IV

~ Message: Bottle #32

Ignore that last one I sent you.
I'd really rather you didn't
try to find me.

Everything human is perfect here, round,
worn smooth. These green bottles
and the bones beside them.

They clink and shift in the wind.
I take in lame snakes.
Sometimes I sing

and the birds sit up on their branches.
Time is the boomerang of sun.
At night the dark shapes

of island surround me; I remember myself
stupid among you, freeing prisoners
in love with their chains,

always taking, as was the custom, parts
for the whole—the body's cavities for what
they wanted: pupils

for the black opacities they saw through.
The mouth
for what it watered to surround.

❧ Auburn

a moderate brown that is yellower and duller than
toast brown, lighter and slightly yellower than
tobacco, paler and slightly yellower than bay,
redder and slightly lighter and stronger than
chestnut brown, and redder, lighter, and slightly
stronger than coffee . . .

—*Webster's Third New International Dictionary*

When I tell you that my life now
is generally speaking happier
than it was a year ago,
or even two months ago, though
slightly more complexly fraught
with emotional obstacles of the kind
you don't really mind
on most days—
I mean you'd have to have
been there. At least a year ago.
And you'd want to ask me
to what was that measure
relative? That is, was my childhood
a struggle, did it cost me any effort
to smile when my father called
I'm home! Or didn't he ever
come home?
Has it been easy
to get or achieve things,
and if so which was easier
or which did I care about the most?
When I scrawled things on walls
did I really mean them?
Was I taught to say
attain and *earn*

54

so as to seem less vulgarly
one of the getting?
Did I dread the day
when I'd be asked to take over
the family business? (Shoes?)
Or did I wish my mother
was not a prostitute
who was never home
at night, or an important
scientist or a stewardess?
Was I afraid my parents
would divorce or kill each other
or abandon me, or was I afraid
I was afraid they wouldn't?
Or perhaps my terrors were
the usual Catholic ones.

I think you'd need to know more
to get an accurate impression
of whether this year or week
meets my standard of happiness—
or exceeds it! Possible?
Do I need a quaint house
in Colorado *and* a gorgeous condo
in Chicago, or what?
Do I demand that people
breathe softly when they see me,
My god, she looks stunning!
Men *and* women, or just men?
Just women?
(Do I see that as an oxymoron?)
Am I bitter, does happiness
shock me when I feel it,
or might I mistake it for
mere absentmindedness
or rest? Is disappointment

so naturally a part of my day
that I take a certain vitamin
to counteract its effects?
Do you wish you knew the name
of that vitamin? (No, this is not
irrelevant! The more alike we are,
the greater your capacity to understand
my blisses and burn-outs.
[In fact, I don't see how
I can continue without learning
a little more about yourself.
I need to know what particulars
pertain to your lifestyle
so I can dress my universals
appropriately. Are you an old man
with none of your original teeth
and have you lost hope of seeing
any of your daughters marry
happily? Do they forget to visit
often, or do they often forget
to visit? Does rock 'n roll
disgust you, as it does Frank Zappa,
who says rock musicians just whine
about their own personal tragedies
and who cares when we all have our own?
And where does that leave art?
How much happier were you
when you had teeth? Or do you
just hate the way they spell
rock 'n roll, is it *faux* cuteness
or do you hate the abuse
of woofers and tweeters,
do you wish there were a society
for that? What do you think it takes
to make Frank Zappa happy?])

◢ℰ The Time Between Trains

Ah, Romance . . . Don't talk to *me!*
I guess I've asked for little else.
Still look for it in the cracks
of sidewalks, PETE AND DEBBIE FOR
EVER, the EVER buckling where a tree
has stretched its ancient roots to make
the first pocked irony of youth: *ever*
lasting rarely, or at least not long
after Pete will drop that stick of his.

Oh, you mean Love? Same thing, you say?
To me it's like the difference between
thinking about having a strawberry milkshake
and actually fixing yourself one. No?
You really think I'm past knowing?
These magazines here, they promise
to cure my arthritis and make me look
fifteen years younger. Do I want
to look sixty-five? I had skin like yours.

Romance isn't like love, up front, out loud.
I'd say it's sharper, more secret. Selfish!
Stolen looks, an awe you don't mention.
It's passion so strong we embarrass ourselves,
we need some distance to manage it, or see it.
Listen, when I was your age I'd heard
the riverbanks of Paris *were* romance,
and I went dutifully sniffing along the quais,
hanging over misty rails, breathing in
(I thought) *l'essence vraie de l'amour;*
while real Parisians, our cousin lemmings,
drove themselves to Rome and Venice.
Always to the unknown, where fluent speech
is difficult, or just not necessary.

There was a lesson in that, but still
I fell—fall!—for the cheap appeal
of the remotely picturesque,
the distant distances of stars,
the echo of imagined heels on ancient walkways.
Countless afternoons I spent leaning
at windows of cafés dreaming up men
over the heads of real ones, or over books
that reduce life's million thrills
to spicy repartee and hungry kisses—
Of which I got my share, my fair share . . .

Really I remember none of it so well
as a chilly night in a Métro station:
stained white tiles, fluorescent glare,
the man across the tracks who put his paper down
to watch me shake rain from my hair.

◢ Letter to the Cracker Company

Forgive my clumsy writing, but
I am old. My fingers, and
I used to take pride
but hope you can read this.

I don't eat much, the cat even
ran away. You could see
in her eyes when she looked up
when there wasn't enough.

But I still buy them still
three blocks away, not far
but when you are old
it is a long way to go

to return crackers
when they are crumbled
when I open the package
already all crumbled

and my table is small
so a lot spills on the floor
and now even the cat.
I know it's not your fault

sometimes crushed on delivery
trucks or the shelf but my table
is small and I am too old
to take anything back.

ᔥ Good for a Girl

Boy, we got into scrapes back then
And I'm not talking knees, though yours
Were always scuffed with real blood.
We terrorized the sitters, scared
The pants off the neighborhood boys.
They knew you were the mastermind:
My main obligation was to cry
When it looked like we were caught,
And all the naughty words we knew
You'd stolen from the walls and desks
Good girls were not supposed to see,
Sliding curses off your tongue
With snide aplomb, the way you sealed
Our thank-you notes for sissy gifts:
Charm bracelets, sachets, lacy socks.

Hey, that's pretty good for a girl,
The boys slurred through wads of Bazooka
When you were first to shinny up
The tallest tree on the block—in shorts!—
To get robin's eggs they shrugged at
But wanted more than you did. Me,
I was always two and a half
short steps behind and still in the way,
I didn't care! I didn't! Headlong
After you I flew from low roofs
And unsteady swings, tossing my heart
To your wilder tune, your shaggy boyfriends,
The posters you hung. But there was nothing
I could offer that you hadn't
Already bitten big chunks from.
Did you ever cry your heart out?
I never heard you through the door.

The night I opened mine you taught me
To dilute tears with expensive scotch
(*Your head won't hurt tomorrow, whatever
Else does*), scoffing, reviling the bastards.
You covered for me the deeper debts
A brotherless youth can lead to.

*   *

For a full grown-up month I had to watch you
Strapped to that sweaty plank in the hospital—
Bruised, bound, gagged, sucking air from a straw
And rasping for ice, for a milkshake, for some peace
For Chrissake, writing weakly in a lurchy
Fourth-grade hand, losing years with each pint,
Behaving like a child for the first time ever
In my guarded eyes. I hardly spoke.
Live   Live   Live   I wanted to be shouting
As you winced and smirked and blamed the nurses
For the dangling respirator you'd ripped out
Yourself, *You can do it* I wanted to holler
While you mocked me for being scared like always,
Scared and still biting my thumb on the sidelines,—
Live I couldn't cry out as you fixed death
With a stare it couldn't return, until at last
It swore and shrugged and spat and shuffled off
Like all the stupid boys you'd ever struck out,
Backing away: *Go on and live*, it said
And so did I, but shyly, under my breath,
Since it was at your battered knee
And from your bleeding lip I learned to.

The Dropping of a Name

It figures. Someone I remember not knowing
unearths the one lousy part of myself
I'd found a decent hole for. My real name
comes to you like a strand of hair
snagged on the edge of your desk.
Can you blame me? I'd change names
like sheets if the law would allow it.
Jack cut down an entire beanstalk,
and no one complained. Say that my giant
was short, or only human. My horror
outgrew him; it's what I remember
of what I'd undo.
And what's that to you?

Nothing personal, but sometimes one's past
is. E.g., an old lover's face reappearing
like a smear, a sticky intrusion:
a tar bubble popping from the repaved
layers of self you tread from one day
to the next, lifting your feet just enough
to keep moving, tracing the patchy ruts
with a crusty sole—the ginger delight
in such pastness! and letting it graze
only the rougher edges of your presence:
a temporary dent in a callus.
Tiny bubble splattering black
on one wingless heel.

Look, I want you to know I'm not weird
or anything. I cross only wadable rivers,
and keep the old fingertips. Still . . .
And I'll grant you: fancy meeting you here,
our antlers locked in the same dream!

Never mind. What did you and I exchange
but a volley of rolled eyes? Or share,
but a simultaneous sip of the same
awful batch of coffee? Your version
of one day, say October, a Tuesday, nineteen-
something, might well ruin mine.
Perhaps I *can* recall the same
wet-sneaker smell, the blood of an Englishman
mixing with yellow marker. Fie on it!
Fo-Fum! I'd remember nothing of the old rooms
but how I got out of them.

If the others should ask, tell them you only
thought you saw me, quickly walking away:
spitting image of no one you knew.

✒ Remains

It never fails to astonish us:
the shyness of flamboyant friends,
the daredevil's fear of heights,
the strong man's fear of other
strong men. But it makes sense.
What we most dread to show
determines half of what we do.

Once a boy whose right arm
had been withered by polio
lifted me with his left
like a sheaf of paper,
carried me easily over
half an acre of mud, and later
became a lifeguard,
drove a stick shift.
I've read of stutterers
who became newscasters, lawyers,
or so adept at finding synonyms
and changing the subject
we'd never guess what words
they never say.

I've found it naked in the works
of sages: shock-white pearls,
maxims from the purple mantle
of untold mistakes. And listen
to me—you may detect the rigid
tone that creeps into the tone
I take when my ex-husband calls,
vocal cords thickening like fibers
of scar tissue to protect
the deeper, torn muscle.
And in the life I've learned

to think I like: the terror
of loneliness compelling all
these years of practice
at being comfortably alone . . .

And you, *semblable*, silent partner,
looking perhaps for confessions
to obviate your own,
or for something you're afraid to be
missing, something we share.

All I know is they're still here,
deficiencies we strove to overcome,
weaknesses we burn to be rid of.
The penniless dreams of a millionaire.
The remains of a murderer's love.

A NOTE ON THE POET

J. Allyn Rosser was born in Bethlehem, Pennsylvania, in 1957, and educated at Middlebury College and the University of Pennsylvania, where she is currently a doctoral candidate. She has received a number of awards, including the Frederick Bock Prize from *Poetry* and a fellowship from the New Jersey State Council on the Arts. Her poems have appeared in *The Georgia Review*, *The Hudson Review*, *Paris Review*, and *Poetry*, among other journals and anthologies.

A NOTE ON THE PRIZE

The Samuel French Morse Poetry Prize was established in 1983 by the Northeastern University Department of English in order to honor Professor Morse's distinguished career as teacher, scholar, and poet. The members of the prize committee are Francis C. Blessington, Joseph deRoche, Victor Howes, Stuart Peterfreund, and Guy Rotella.